Dinosaur School

DINOSAUR OPPOSITES

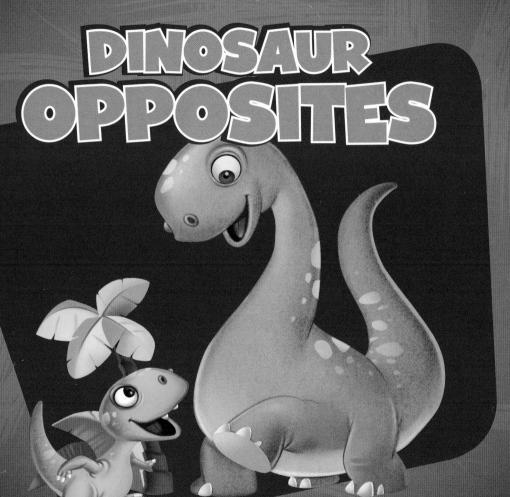

Please visit our website, www.garethstevens.com. For a free color catalog of all our high-quality books, call toll free 1-800-542-2595 or fax 1-877-542-2596.

Library of Congress Cataloging-in-Publication Data

Saviola, Ava.
Dinosaur opposites / Ava Saviola.
    p. cm. — (Dinosaur school)
ISBN 978-1-4339-7144-0 (pbk.)
ISBN 978-1-4339-7145-7 (6-pack)
ISBN 978-1-4339-7143-3 (library binding)
1. Dinosaurs—Juvenile literature. 2. Polarity—Juvenile literature. I. Title.
QE861.5.S34495 2013
567.9—dc23

                        2011044296

First Edition

Published in 2013 by
Gareth Stevens Publishing
111 East 14th Street, Suite 349
New York, NY 10003

Copyright © 2013 Gareth Stevens Publishing

Designer: Ben Gardner
Editor: Kerri O'Donnell

All illustrations by Planman Technologies

Printed in the United States of America

CPSIA compliance information: Batch #CS12GS: For further information contact Gareth Stevens, New York, New York at 1-800-542-2595.

DINOSAUR OPPOSITES

By Ava Saviola

Gareth Stevens
Publishing

big

small

long

short

up

down

near

far

heavy

light

in

out

happy

sad

day

night

hot

cold

loud

quiet

Dinosaur Opposites

big

small

long

short

up

down

near

far

heavy

light

in

out

happy

sad

day

night

hot

cold

loud

quiet

24